FIRE SAFETY

WITH LIEUTENANT TOBY!

WRITTEN BY ED SCHNEYER JR.

ILLUSTRATED BY JOHN DLUG

For my mom, who taught me
the value of family and how to write a poem,
and whose Pasta Sundays always bring me home.

For my dad, who taught me
to be a jack of all trades and work hard for good grades,
and that I could achieve any goal that I made.

- E.S.

Anyone who has encouraged me to continue doing the things I love,
despite all challenges, thank you.

- J.D.

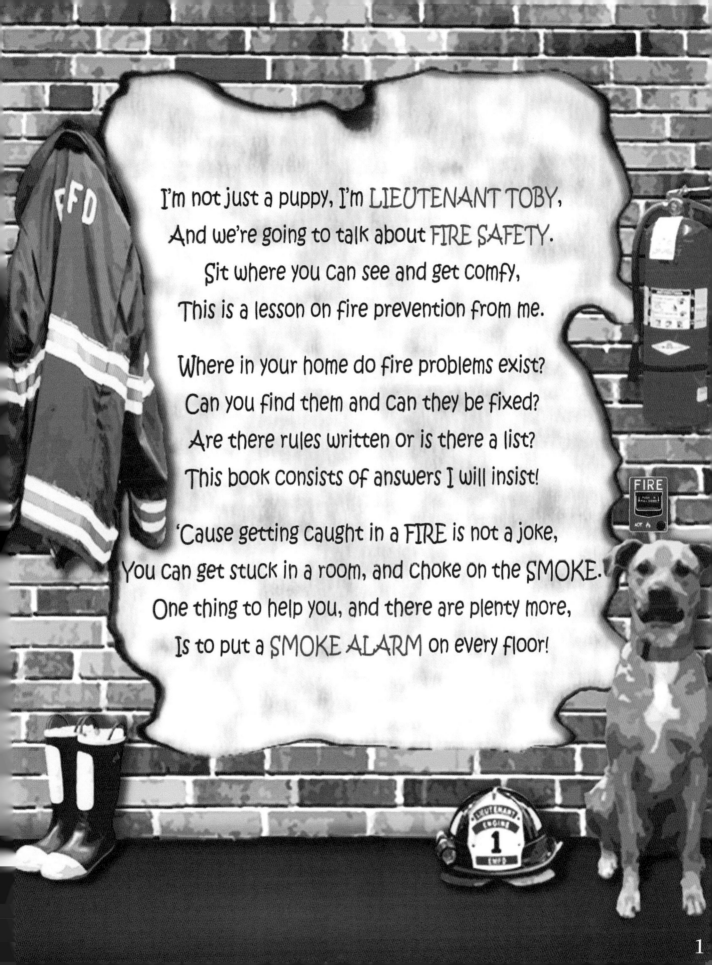

I'm not just a puppy, I'm LIEUTENANT TOBY,
And we're going to talk about FIRE SAFETY.
Sit where you can see and get comfy,
This is a lesson on fire prevention from me.

Where in your home do fire problems exist?
Can you find them and can they be fixed?
Are there rules written or is there a list?
This book consists of answers I will insist!

'Cause getting caught in a FIRE is not a joke,
You can get stuck in a room, and choke on the SMOKE.
One thing to help you, and there are plenty more,
Is to put a SMOKE ALARM on every floor!

SMOKE ALARMS work while you're catching ZZZ's,
They detect smoke that can be five hundred degrees.
They warn you EARLY, of an emergency,
So getting CAUGHT in a fire will be half as likely!

But if your alarm's NOT working properly,
You may NOT act immediately.
Make it a priority, to MONTHLY check every BATTERY,
And you and your family may be injury free!

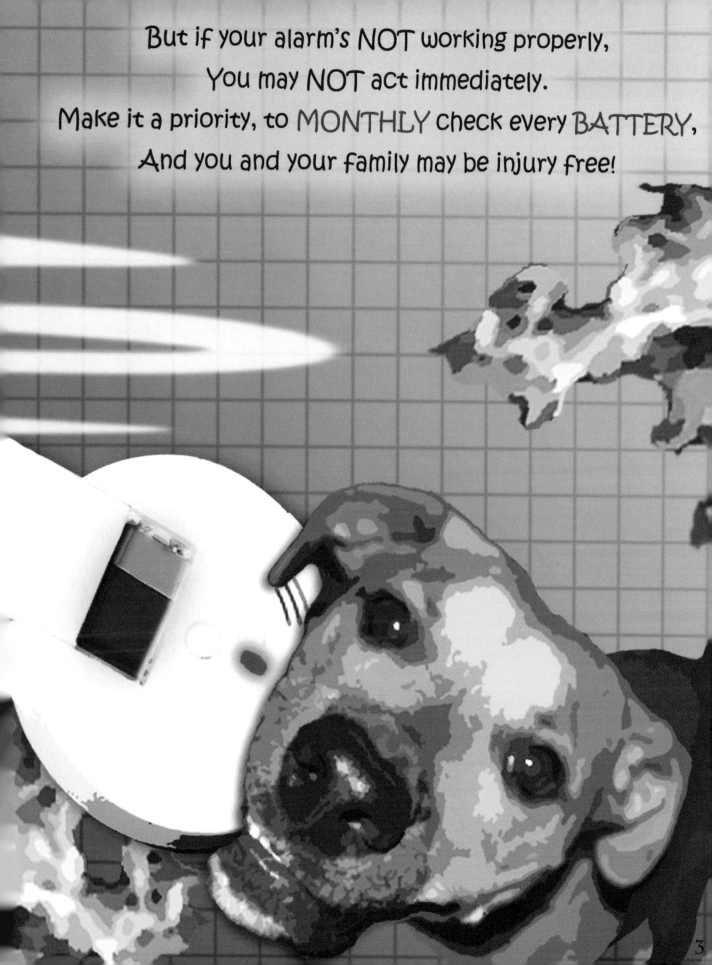

If you hear your smoke alarm - you should know beforehand,
Always CRAWL to the door - you NEVER want to stand.
Feel the top of the door with the back of your hand,
If it's HOT don't open - or the fire EXPANDS!

When it comes to an EXIT PLAN - have no doubt,
Every room in the house should have TWO ways out.
If a fire BLOCKS the door just take another route,
Get to the FAMILY MEETING PLACE outside the house!

I'll say it again,
But I've said it before.
Make sure there's a smoke alarm
On every floor!

Once you've made it OUT -
You NEVER go back in,
That's the job for the trained FIREMEN.
They'll get there quick with SIRENS and then,
They'll use their skills,
To save ANYONE within!

If you're UPSTAIRS, when the fire appears,
DON'T FEAR -
Make noise for firefighters to hear.
WINDOWS can be exits, so make sure that they're CLEAR,
They may be the ONLY way out,
If a fire is near!

Fires can spread,
As FAST as you run.
Don't WASTE time,
Saving toys that are fun.
Get OUT of the house,
And YOU be the one,
To pick up a phone and

Dial 9-1-1!

8

FIRE EXTINGUISHERS at home should be easy to see,
You should know the difference between A, B, and C.
Learn how to PULL the pin free and then aim correctly,
And be sure to call the F.D. immediately!

ORDINARY

A - Trash · Wood · Paper

COMBUSTIBLES

FLAMMABLE

B - Liquids · Grease

LIQUIDS

ELECTRICAL

C - Electrical Equip.

EQUIPMENT

I'll say it again,
But I've said it before.
Make sure there's a smoke alarm
On every floor!

The KITCHEN is the place where MOST fires occur,
An extinguisher HERE is what you prefer.
NEVER leave food cooking to do things faster,
A spark or a splatter can cause a DISASTER!

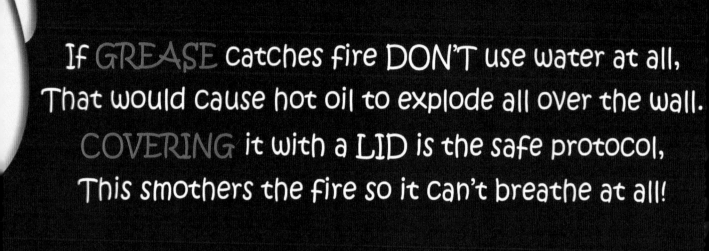

If GREASE catches fire DON'T use water at all,
That would cause hot oil to explode all over the wall.
COVERING it with a LID is the safe protocol,
This smothers the fire so it can't breathe at all!

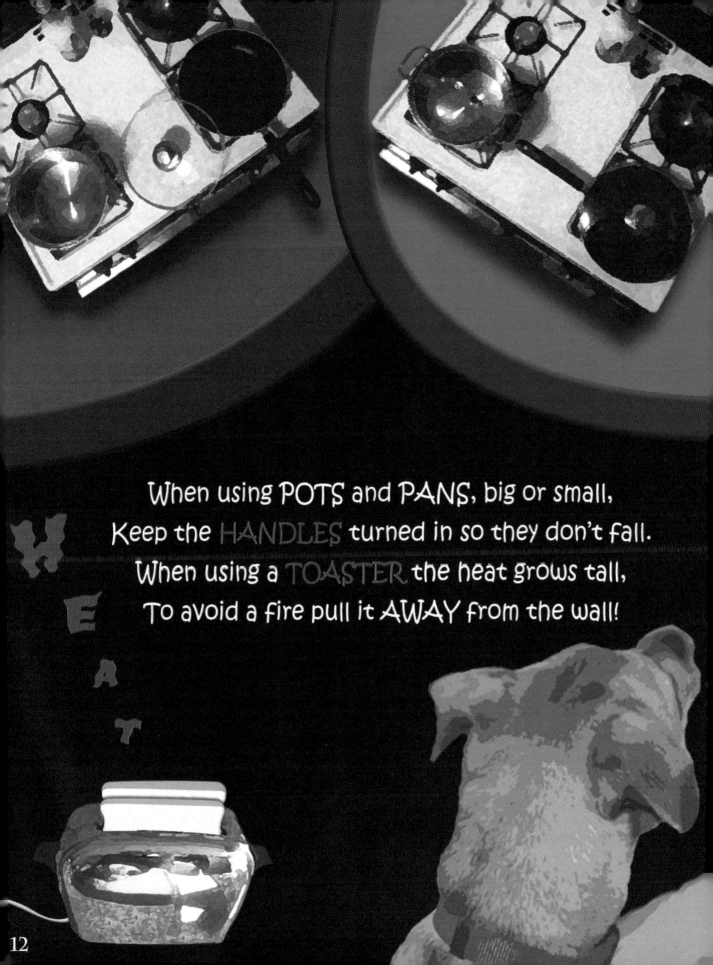

When using POTS and PANS, big or small,
Keep the HANDLES turned in so they don't fall.
When using a TOASTER the heat grows tall,
To avoid a fire pull it AWAY from the wall!

When using a MICROWAVE,
You can get burned,

If you've pulled plates out quickly,
You've probably learned.

Hot STEAM may rise,
When the covers unturned,

Don't put METAL in microwaves,
That's a red flag of concern!

I'll say it again,
But I've said it before.
Make sure there's a smoke alarm
On every floor!

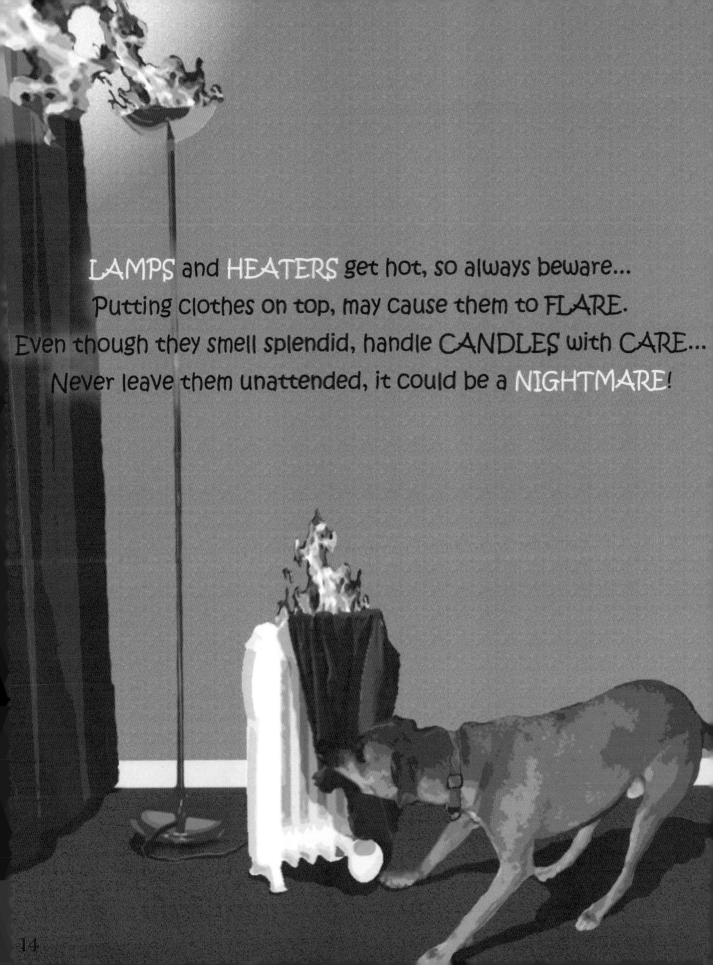

LAMPS and HEATERS get hot, so always beware...
Putting clothes on top, may cause them to FLARE.
Even though they smell splendid, handle CANDLES with CARE...
Never leave them unattended, it could be a NIGHTMARE!

14

If using CANDLES, make sure there's an adult in the room,
And even then you should never assume.
When candles are lit, trouble ALWAYS may loom,
A swing of my tail can make them go BOOM!

OVERLOADING an outlet with too many wires,
Can cause a SHORTAGE and even a fire.
UNPLUGGING appliances when done is required,
And never LEAVE home while running the dryer!

16

Fires can start as quick as a blink,
So keep ELECTRICAL WIRES out of the SINK.
When using EXTENSION CORDS - stop and think,
DON'T run them under rugs, and check for cracks and kinks!

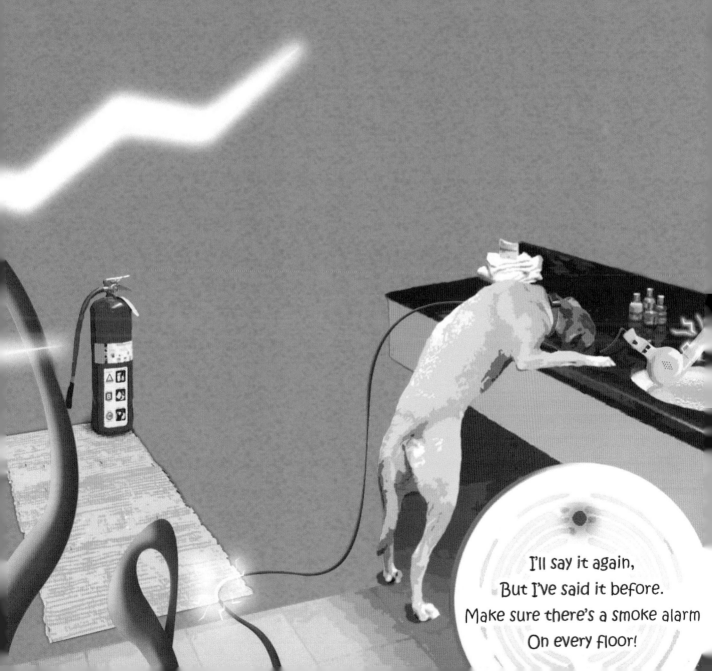

I'll say it again,
But I've said it before.
Make sure there's a smoke alarm
On every floor!

DON'T play with matches, you know the rules,
MATCHES and LIGHTERS are NOT toys, they're TOOLS.
You've probably learned this every year when in school,
If you find them, tell an adult and you will be COOL!

If your clothes catch fire you should know your role,
Running makes the fire burn out of CONTROL.
COVER your face and make it your goal,
To always remember to STOP, DROP and ROLL!

There is another ALARM every home should contain,
And a CARBON MONOXIDE detectors the name.
It should be placed near all BEDROOM domains,
Get OUT if it sounds - never play any games!

BEEP
BEEP
BEEP
BEEP

Family Meeting
Place

Carbon Monoxide (CO) and smoke are NOT the same,
CO causes trouble before you feel pain.
It's colorless, odorless and may be there without flames,
And it SILENTLY blocks OXYGEN from your brain!

I'll say it again,
But I've said it before.
Make sure there's a smoke alarm
On every floor!

FIREFIGHTERS never fear if the fire's severe,
They train all year, and they wear the right gear.
Whether paid or VOLUNTEER, they're brave and sincere.
And they'll PERSEVERE, until the fire disappears!

After reading this book you must agree,
You should CHECK your home, and fix the problems you see.
SMOKE ALARMS that work properly, are most important to me.
And EXIT PLANS with FAMILY MEETING PLACES are key!

If you follow these rules, the safer you'll be.
If there is a fire at home, you should KNOW where to be.
If you forget what to do - just check back with me,
LIEUTENANT TOBY, the EXPERT on FIRE SAFETY!

Made in the USA
Lexington, KY
27 October 2014